Managing Accounts Receivable: How 54 Sales Professionals Collect Past Due Accounts

Category: Business & Economics

Description: While having a small accounts-receivable balance indicates good financial management, collecting past-due balances is a difficult aspect of the sales process. Any delay in collecting past-due accounts will reduce your chance of receiving payment. Fifty-four sales professionals share their strategy with you.

Key words: past due receivables, collect accounts receivable, accounts receivable collection, collect overdue accounts, sales and receivables.

Copyright Bob Oros-2014

ISBN 978-1-312-94017-8

Written and published by Bob Oros

832 NW 142nd Street, Edmond, OK 73013

Ph 405-751-9191 Email Bob@BobOros.com

Web site www.BobOros.com

ISBN 978-1-312-94017-8

90000

9 781312 940178

About the author

Regardless of whether you are reading one of his books or attending one of his presentations, the most frequent comment is: "This guy has been there, he is one of us, I am going to use these strategies." With over 2,000 presentations in all 50 states and as far away as New Zealand, as well as being a CSP (Certified Speaking Professional, the highest designation awarded by the National Speakers Association and the International Federation for Professional Speakers), you can feel confident you will get the results you are looking for.

Ron Meyers:

My suggestion is that the seller can use exactly the words you used--Here's how you can "help me help you!"--and in doing so make the seller and the buyer into a team together trying to resolve the problem of late payment instead of a confrontation between two adversaries--one who is late paying and the other who wants payment soon.

Bill Messer:

Let them know that you only get paid one time a month and it is based on the money you collected and not what you sold. So if you don't collect it will be another month before you will be paid for what you sold

Tom Wheat:

I have found that texting is less confrontational than a phone call. A phone call can sometimes catch a customer at a busy time or a bad time. A text can be read at any time. This only works with customers that are going to pay but just need a little prodding. It also indicates that if you don't get a response you are probably going to follow up with a phone call. They know they owe the invoices and a text indicates that now is the time to pay or at least respond to a text. If you don't get a response it is time to withhold shipment or place on C.O.D. before you get more unpaid invoices.

Ian Edwards:

I make sure that my terms of business (i.e. payment) are included in any and all proposals.

At the point of receiving an order, I ask the buyer to tell me who is involved in the payment process and their contact details.

My invoices include all the information and latest day for payment.

I send the invoice by post or email (whichever they prefer) to the main contact in the customers' accounts departments and then phone to ensure that they have received it and have everything they need to pay me. At the same time I obtain confirmation of the date they will be paying me, reminding them of my agreed terms of business if the date offered is beyond my terms

If payment is not received on the agreed date, I phone to check that payment has been sent

When payment is received on time, I send a thank you card to thank the accounts department for processing my payment promptly. This action alone puts me at the top of their list for paying me first the next   time they purchase from me.

Trip English:

I treat collections as a "grade' with accounts:

I will print out their A/R each week and circle any invoices past due and depending on the extent, write a "D-" or "C+" on their page in red ink. The next week when their A/R is current, I will print a new sheet with an "A+" on it. You will be surprised how this is an ice breaker, everyone wants a good grade!

Michael Juell:

From a Food Sales perspective, there was an A/R balance I had to collect to keep them current. There was the optional payment plan.

As an Independent Consultant, I require a 50% fee upfront, with the remainder due on delivery.

I do take trade, payment plans. I even do the work and have a verbal agreement to pay in 60 days, so far I haven't had a problem.

David Williams:

Try not to take a hard line with customers. If you approach it with the attitude of helping the customer, you seem to get a lot further with them. I have set up customers with paying a certain amount extra every week so they don't have to take a big hit all at once. Usually if you ask for an extra invoice paid every week, they feel they can handle that and don't feel to pressured.

Jason R. Boekholder:

I find that when a situation gets tough explain to a customer that he purchased the product at a fair price, sold it for a profit and we have every right to collect what he has already made a profit on it.

"Doc" Willy Hughes:

As you know, in sales, every solution can be as unique as each relationship... but a technique that I use for more delicate situations is to put my customer into the "advisor's seat" (this can work for collections, penetration, etc.)...

I build my customer's confidence by letting them know how much I respect their business savvy or experience, or knowledge and then I ask their advise on how they would deal with the situation at hand.. some times I even use a "some other customer" scenario ....most times they usually give me enough insights as to how to solve our little situation that it usually keeps our relationship intact and even stronger coming out the other side."

Frank Rhodes:

1) Go into account over and over just to collect.

2) Sit down and have a frank discussion with client to discuss what is and isn't possible for both companies involved.

a) Try to come up with a plan that is real and workable for everyone.

3) Take money out of the register, in front of client.

4) Take out coffee and tea equipment.

5) Quit delivering to them.

6) Before these things work out COD or COD Cash when approved by Credit Department.

7) Go to Credit Department for suggestions.

8) Mainly continue to think about some kind of solution, unless customer is taking advantage of you on purpose (which is rare).

Larry J Malone:

In order to help any slow pays, I've always tried to get them to set up payments along with new invoices and pay all new invoices on time to avoid late charges which the company enforces which in the contract they signed as most contracts have in these times. I suggest this will take care of the problem without being cutoff and publicized in a lawsuit and judgments. If they will do this It will make me look good with my bosses and I can always get a rush order or any other problem that may arise completed for them without my bosses throwing slow pay in my face.

If they'll help me it will help them which makes our relationship continue as a great friendship as well as a client / sales person relation. We'll both give and take to help one another.

Most companies won't treat their clients this as their accounting control this area and unless a sales person makes it their duty to find out this is happening and prevent it before the acct. dept. cuts the client off of future service or product and you find out too late. I haven't lost but a couple of clients and they refused to work with me also, so I ended up closing them myself.

Tony Treser:

Quite often we will make the Bank the "Bad Guy" and tell our customer that the Bank will not allow us to issue additional credit or the Bank will force us to file a legal suit.

Also we have found credit insurance to be quite affordable and allow us to be more aggressive with some of the accounts we pursue.

Tina Haugland:

The best way we deal with slow paying customers has always been upfront. Don't away from the conversation and keep it part of the daily business routine. It helps us our pricing in line and improves the working relationship. Thanks

Robin Chambers:

Any new accounts I opened with no more than 7 days and we review to increase it after 5 weeks of scheduled payments to 14 days then another 5 weeks to 21 days. If payments are made on this schedule with no problems then I have assisted the account greatly. Very few begin anew with 30 days D.O.I. I state to the client that this is to assist them to keep a tight handle on their cost.

The best plan I have is not to shy away form the situation. I get the accounts payable officers e-mail, phone number and work them, not avoiding the Chef but going to the decision maker or the person who has the owners ear ASAP. I assure all concerned that we are here to assist with this situation and have my accounts receivable officer involved as well. I forward their aging weekly with invoice numbers, date of invoices and amounts due.

Most important I enforce our relationship as working partners with the Chef and separate the accounting from he daily equation

Warren Coughlin:

One technique that works is the "helpful assistant" approach. On day 28, the assistant calls and says "Listen, I've been told that we are going to start levying the interest charges on late accounts. I see yours still hasn't come in. I'm doing the processing, so if you can get it to me in the next 5 days, I'll be able to put it through without the interest levy."

Another is just the upfront positioning. Ensure payment terms are agreed upon. (Not foolproof by any stretch, but if you get them squirming, you can ask what their payment terms are and get them to agree to that. At least you have knowledge of when to expect.)

Serena Goulish:

I think it is important to set the foundation for payment expectations from the onset of doing business. One should not assume there is a mutual understanding of expectations.

Having worked for 12+ years in sales for a broad line food distributor I learned not to shy away from the topic. First step is to meet the person or people who actually pay the bills and get their email address for ease of communication.

Every customer is handled differently and the sooner an understanding of what is expected is established the better.

Gary Stuart:

I know I have a few real problems. Short of me writing their check, I don't know how else to handle them. Maybe this exercise will help. Here's what I currently do:

I tell them I have a serious problem. I tell them how much and how far they are past due. I ask if they have recently sent in a check, and how much, that maybe has not yet been posted. I really appreciate their business, but I need them to get caught up to under 21 days. If they do that, I'll never ask about money again. The credit dept. and management are on my back to get them caught up. I tell them that they would much rather hear from me than the credit dept. More than likely, he will put them on COD, and would be a real hassle to them if that happened. I also tell them I don't get paid the commission until the invoice is paid. Almost always, I get the answer, "I will get it caught up". I will tell them I understand if they can't pay all at once, but please try within the next 2 weeks. Always get an "ok".

Bob Dougherty:

One of the statements that I tell a customer that is behind on payments, is that it takes away from the leverage that I have with my company, of giving them special prices, or deals on items that are

Sensitive to their business. I tell them that the company can't justify good prices , to someone that is not staying with in their terms. And if they lose these deals it could take a long time to get them back, If they ever will.

Chuck Mastruserio:

As a sales rep for the company I work for I feel that it's an important aspect of my job to keep the Aging Report current. Depending on the exact situation, I approach the process in steps.

Step 1 with accounts payable. "I need your help. Something may have been overlooked" How can we correct this for you?

Step 2. There seems to be another glitch. We need to correct this now what do you suggest?

Step 3. Use your company policy to proceed as the incentive before it actually comes down to utilizing it. " I'm sorry per your suggestion we've tried XYZ but it didn't seem to work before we need to (insert policy here) I'll need a check number, payment, reason for deduction etc...

Don't be bashful, overly forceful, or half informed with the facts. Have all the pertinent information and facts (invoice numbers, check numbers bill back totals etc) on hand and be ready to explain that as needed. A matter of fact approach works well for me. Accounting folks love lots of back up! The more precise you are the quicker the issue will be resolved.

Randy Johnson:

One way is every time you see the customer bring a snap shot of the Open Invoice Report of what they have on the books and find a way to show them the report by easing into the conversation, usually within a few weeks to a few months they get used to you bringing it to their attention, I've even been known to remind a few customers that they never seem to have a problem asking me to bend over backwards for them by making extra deliveries or will call's when they forget to order something and so it should not be a problem for them to remember to keep up their end of the bargain and pay their bill on time.

Jane Sands:

I am NOT a real person!   BUT, clients who haven't paid our accounts don't know this!

I'm a "made-up" name.   I do not exist. We do this because it makes collecting any unpaid accounts much less confrontational, allows the debtor to "save face", and leaves the creditor as someone who's trying to help, not hassle.

How does it work?

1.   Any 'please-pay' emails or letters are sent out under my (?!) name as soon as an account is overdue,

2.   All that a 'real' person then has to say when making a "collection" phone call is "Hi John. My accounts people are chasing me up about one of your invoices.   Can you help?"

3.   And then just listen; after blaming ME (!!) for having to make the call.

And I'm not a real person. Sounds ridiculous, but it works ... extremely well!

Dominick Yarnal:

Collecting money is probably the hardest and most difficult part of a sales job. Every situation is different, from payment terms, 7days,COD, monthly...., to who actually pays and how they pay.

I always discussed this when I open the account, and actually have it written down in a hand out I give to all new customers, which also includes delivery schedule, contacts and office numbers...Most of my customer know that they owe me as soon as I walk in the door. Although some reluctantly. I also emphasize the fact that I don't get paid until they pay there bill. You're always going to get a few who push it until the last possible term, but the majority know they owe and try to pay.

Chris Brown;

My attempts to moving slow paying customers to good customers has been a roller coaster ride over the years. Here are some ways I have dealt with slow payers.

I have tried every angle I can to help move people into paying faster. I have just hounded them about money every time I have seen them. (this works for some). I have raised their prices until they say something, which gave me a chance to explain how money works. (this works with some) I have put letters of promise together for the customer to agree to in writing with weekly goals they promise to pay.(this one is one of the more successful) I have had quarterly business and weekly A/R reviews that alone has some success in collections, I guess what I am saying is this….any plan to combat slow payers into collections works, you have to ask for the money.

Denny Luellen:

One way I deal with slow paying customers is by telling them that people above me that watch or accounts receivable when it goes past due will automatically go to COD.

Dan DiStefano:

The one thing I have always told my customers for the last 14+ years is; "I can help you in every way possible and I can give you a great price, as long as you're not past due. I have very few slow paying customers for one reason; you have to train them from the start. I can't afford to be wasting my time running around colleting checks.

Mark Haskins:

One technique for collections that works for me once a customer gets behind their terms is a payment plan. We agree on the past due balance amount and spread the payments over a 5-10 week period. They customer agrees to stay current with future shipments and pay the balance off in mutually agreed upon smaller chunks on a weekly basis. This fosters a sense of partnership with the customer.

Ken Goodwin:

With the economic challenges we are faced with it is critical that we keep our customers current with their payment terms; for their sakes and ours. We preach this consistently to our people. Not only because of the credit risk an out-of-terms account poses but also for the damage to the selling relationship that occurs as a result of poor collections. Customers who are behind in their bills tend to avoid their creditors at the expense of a healthy business relationship.

I've heard a story on numerous occasions about a former sales rep from one of our branches who did not proceed with the sales call until after he collected the amount due on his customer's account. His customers knew that he expected to get paid and they came to the table with their checkbook in hand. If he did not receive the payment due he would pack up his laptop and refused to take their next order. He almost always got paid and he consistently had the lowest bad debt and out-of-terms customers in the organization. Now, this didn't happen overnight but he did over time create an expectation that he was going to get timely payments for the goods and services he provided. By the way, this particular sales rep was one of our top sales performers as well.

Stuart Gray:

UFDA is the acronym that I use in establishing a new business relationship.

Up Front Defining Agreement

The rules of payment are established prior to doing any business. By explaining to the new customer that I am in the sales growth business not collections! If they want to exceed last year's results, our time needs to be spent on business growth discussions, not payment!

Once the rules are established and mutuality agreed upon then it is really easy to focus the sales call on productive behavior. It is then up to the sales professional to respect and honor the sales call.

Van Laughlin:

I have always found the only way to deal with the collection process is to make it just like the rest of your sales call. Print out a collection report, bring it with you on the call and underline or highlight the amount that needs to be picked up and THE DATE you need it. Explain that credit is getting harder to deal with situations especially with the state of the economy. I personally believe that if it's a situation you need to get management involved immediately.

Bob Knight:

Even though no two customers are alike, they all realize the importance staying current. I try to express to my accounts that the true meaning of a independent business person is owning the inventory in their backroom. Staying within terms makes things a lot easier.

John Hillistor:

The way I deal with potential slow pays is to say that COD customers get the best price. I work in seasonal areas and since my company goes out to monthly credit terms or 28 day I explain that after season those big bills will keep rolling in even though the customers are not. I try to have most customers on no more than 14 day terms. It seems the monthly accounts find a way to hang themselves with the credit terms.

James S Jones:

The first step to keeping your collections in line is to identify the customers that need special attention, second is to have a plan and at least two options for payments planned ahead.

For example Mr. customer as you can see your account is 5 day's past due ,(I always speak in days outstanding before bring up actual dollar amounts, customer seem less passionate about days than cash) in order to bring your account current we need $ (usually I include the invoices that will be come past due in the time it takes to mail, cash and post this payment). Once the customer states he can not accomplish this I then offer a second figure (which normally will prevent us from slipping any further behind) .

Jim Chill:

This is tricky subject, for me it depends on the customer. For Jeff and our accountant it does not matter who the customer is, if a customer is out of terms we aggressively work to get the balance collected. I am very close with many of the Chefs/Owners I work with, for these customers I am more patient if they are outside of terms but only to a certain point. If I have had multiple conversations with them and I still have not received a check I request to Jeff that we not ship another order and possibly resign the business.

For the customers that I don't have a relationship with I am not as lenient. As soon as a customer is out of terms I aggressively work to get a payment. I do this through phone calls and personal visits.

Typically a payment is always received if the customer is communicating with me about when a payment will be made. I get worried when I have no communication from the customer. If I don't receive any feedback I immediately have Jeff deactivate the account.

I think the most important thing to remember is that a company can go out of business if stuck with unpaid bills. The best way to defend against this is to be strict on the terms that are given from the beginning and do credit checks before giving terms, this is probably the best way to prevent a slow pay from happening.

Anonymous:

Make a review of the AR a part of every call. Whether the account is current or not, be sure to make it a habit to have a discussion of AR status as a regular and consistent part of your routine.

Always thank the customers for his business and payment.

Charles D Nolidin:

Structure one of the terms and conditions of the invoice to state that a weekly compounding interest of certain % of the total due amount will be charged after due date. Just like credit charge payment.

Michael Kuhny:

Be honest with them and be honest with yourself.

I ask myself, "Are the services I am providing of value to my slow paying customer?" If yes, then: Tell your customer why you need payment in a more timely fashion. Advise them that if you are unable to collect the money that they owe you that it will adversely affect the services you are providing to them. It usually enhances our relationship.

If no, then find a payment plan that they can adhere to and look at the possibility of either COD or not having them as a customer any longer.

Wes Bartlett:

I like the offer of using a credit card for sales invoice deductions. They generally are on a once a month payment, which allows anyone needing a slower payment program.

Most times you can get the frequent flyer mileage type of card as well.

Ron Sonedecker:

1 Print out customer detail on a timely basis

2 Have several self-addressed, stamped envelops on hand to put checks in and mail nightly

3 Take advantage of your ability to request customer A/R detail

4 Ask for the Money, be the squeaky wheel

5 Be a financial consultant and help the customer with proper documentation

6 Eliminate your fears of approaching the credit issues by using terms like "I need your help Mr. customer in solving these issues" How can I help?

7 Develop or re-develop good customer relationships

8 Have a plan and documentation before going into the account

9 Make collections part of your daily routine (be consistent)

10 Compliment customers that are in terms so if the time arises they are not, discussing A/R will not seem foreign to them.

11 Control information customer is receiving i.e. statements

12 Communicate-Communicate-Communicate with the customer and our credit department

13 Understand credit terms

14 Learn how the customer perceives competitive terms they are using

15 Write credits daily

16 Discuss accounts that are high maintenance, low margin and constantly past due with your DM

17 Set parameters and agreement when setting up the account or when initially taking over an account

18 Fax A/R detail to specific customers on Sunday and a COMMUNICATE when check will be picked up

Dave Ferren:

Slow paying customers have either two issues. One is lack of money or are disorganized with their money. The other is a control issue. People who don't have any money can either turn it around or they can't. Usually these people need structure so give it to them. Give them the parameters and hold them to it. No money—no product. Usually this will get it straight. They don't want an interruption in service because it only adds to the chaos. If they can't get it together then they never will.

Customers who have control issues are very different. IF they pay on time then they are "not" in control. If they pay when they want to then they are " in control". If you don't ship them then they will go somewhere else because the need to be in control is greater than anything else, the product, the service, the relationship with you—anything. If they are worth the time and the margin is good I will stroke their egos. If they aren't I cut them off and move on. I always give them options so they still feel in control. I tell them it is up to them. Silence is the indicator that they have hit the wall. The ones who will not conform to any expectations are never going to with you or anybody else.

Gary Caudill:

The basic terms of trade between us and our customers is determined by our credit department, at our corporate office. We rely on the potential customer to provide as much detail (current vendors, bank name, ect) as possible, for us to contact and verify performance history as it pertains to payments on account.

We usually are very incredulous, so we start out with "short" terms, and after we have our own history of payments, we start to extend terms if needed.

Our ideal scenario would be to get them to pay with a credit-card.

John Myers:

Every customer is different and different techniques need to be implemented for each situation. But...The easiest way to get payment is to tell the customer that their pricing and your service is dependent on the customer paying on time..if not,... pricing will go up...service will drop...and the competition will find out their dilemma through a credit check...and it will be the same story there.

Anette Booth:

I just say: "Will you have a check for me tomorrow?"

Jeff Barnett:

My territory is rural and consists of about 50 customers. My annual sales are in excess of 2 Million.

Fortunately I have very few problems with the customers in my territory because I treat it like a function of my sales call. The majority of my customers pay without me asking but a few I need to keep working with. This is what I do; every morning I print out a statement for the customers that are in question, I then highlight what needs to be paid and discuss it with them at the sales call. I think the reason this works is because they know it is important to me and I am not going to let them slide. If they know I am not paying attention they will go as long as they can without paying. It is up to the sales person to stay on top of things. In today's business it is not just the sales we are responsible for, it is every aspect of our business and the customers business.

Chris Charbonneau:

One of the most helpful tools we have is an automated bank draft. 48 hours after delivery the money is withdrawn from the customer's account. If I could sign everyone up for this I would.

Sharon Shumaker:

We receive, each week, a report that shows where each of our customers are, it is easier to catch them before they get to far out and speak to them about it. If they do get further out they have been warned and then we can take whatever measures each individual account needs. Usually by letting them know that we are on top of, and watching their account they tend to make the effort to catch up.

Tino Larios:

This is the way I deal whit slow payers: I am not afraid to ask for my money. Why do I say "my money?" Because when I set my mind like that it is very easy to confront the costumer. We must protect the company we work for! We are the eyes of our company and unless the company gave you the account then you should be even more careful and thankful to your company. When you are doing your best for your customers they know you deserve to get paid.

Frank Iessi:

My way of dealing with slow paying customers is the way I run my business in general, consistency is the word. I make it a priority to see each customer at as close to the same time each week as possible and the first part of business that we discuss is the customers account. If I receive hesitancy, I explain that to put off paying today will only increase the amount that will be due on my next visit. I try to use the analogy that we are a business that can only operate if we are paid in a timely manner by our customers just like they need to be paid by their customers. I try to help them understand that we will do all we can to help them to succeed, but in order to do this, we need to keep their account in good standing. I hope this helps you in your quest to help other salespeople to make collections a little easier.

Scott Quaranta:

It's a daily battle to keep accounts on time, I use email to start out with sending "what's due this week", then I follow up with a text message confirming the email and letting the customer know I will be by to pick up a check.

This seems to work the best as a starting point

Robbie Blake:

I would ask them how they would like a customer to let them pay next week on the meal they were eating, and when next week comes, ignore paying the bill again and say they could get a meal at another restaurant.

John Lincoln:

Be selective - don't be afraid to turn away business; being desperate and taking anything doesn't pay bills if they do not pay, and the time could be better used in marketing;

~ Drive business to you with articles, newsletters, webinars, etc. I avoid cold calling, but when I used to do it, I got more of those who were payment problems;

~ Build a long-term relationship; like you I like to provide information w/o thought of an immediate pay back;

~ Require a percentage up front (I'm a consultant) -- 1/3 to 1/2 (or more) of a project or a project phase / module;

~ If future payments are dragging .. quit the project w/ explanation and do not take any more from them until past is paid up -- only had one company in this situation; they finally paid and I got some additional work, but the relationship was strained from then on.

Wayne Coutts:

We find a call to our debtors a week before payment is due is a good memory jogger for our customers

We also point out our ability to supply is dependent on their ability to keep their account up to date

Tom Henterly:

Start the customer out on the right foot not the left foot. Be up front with written explanation of their credit terms along with how the payments are paid; be it, by mail, in person, to a driver the answer to fewer problems is to sell the payment process. Most important part of the whole process is telling the customer thank you after each payment is applied.

John Cecala:

For our company we meet with the customer to set up a payment plan to work their outstanding balance into terms. We take new orders COD while they continue to make payments against their balance. In some cases it may take 12 months or longer for them to get caught up.   We feel maintaining the relationship and working with them is better than sending them to collections and severing the relationship totally.

In most cases this works but one has to be careful to ascertain the likelihood they will continue to be in business and be able to make payments.

Anthony Suidan:

I use words like "admin housekeeping", "realized", "status", "update", "please" and "thank you in advance". I list invoice numbers and dates. I prefer email. Email can also be used to drag the electronic correspondence history of date stamps, messages, etc... below it all in one place.

Tim Hankinson:

I ask why they haven't paid?

Is there a problem?

Have we not shipped something?

We need to get this resolved.

Assist them in getting this paid.

I give a target date to get this resolved.

If target date is not hit then they may be on COD.

Laura Knapp:

Persistence is key! First, you must let the client know that you value the relationship & want to keep serving them, but in order to do that they must pay for the goods & services extended to them. Be firm but kind, explaining to the customer that paying just a little extra each week will help catch them up. Letting them know you are there for them, (even dropping by to check in on them outside of your scheduled visits), helps. By staying on top of those customers in a friendly, consistent manner, you prove that they have nothing to dread from your visits & that you are both in it for the long haul.

Once a customer has caught up their balance, "retrain" them to leave a check each time you visit. This worked for me when I inherited some clients who were slow to pay...my A/R numbers improved within two months.

Jim Spencer:

Our attitude is we've got to help keep these people in business so we can get paid over a time frame that works for both the customer & us. We move the old balances into a Promissory Note backed by a Stipulated Confession of Judgment. We charge a very competitive interest rate of 7-9%, & we make every attempt to set the monthly payment so that the customer can afford it but yet high enough to pay off the Note in a timely manner. We run the notes out between 12-36 months.

This has worked exceptionally well for us, & we've been able to get the majority of these customers back on their feet & the notes retired. After all, there aren't too many banks in this economy willing to lend money to finance restaurant receivables right now-especially in California.

We also have a monthly incentive for our sales reps of $200 for receivables greater than 85% current, & $300 for receivables greater than 90% current. The four Regional Sales Managers also get a $500 quarterly incentive if their sales reps average as a team greater than 82% current. We also do one more thing with these customers-if they continue splitting up their business with other distributors & paying them according to their terms, because of our willingness to work with them on their receivables we leverage that & ask for additional business we'd like to gain from them. I hope this helps & I look forward to seeing the summary of what you come up with.

www.ingramcontent.com/pod-product-compliance
Lightning Source LLC
Chambersburg PA
CBHW021905170526
45157CB00005B/1970